Treasure House

Pupil Book 6
Comprehension

Author: Abigail Steel

William Collins' dream of knowledge for all began with the publication of his first book
in 1819. A self-educated mill worker, he not only enriched millions of lives, but also founded
a flourishing publishing house. Today, staying true to this spirit, Collins books are packed
with inspiration, innovation and practical expertise. They place you at the centre of a world
of possibility and give you exactly what you need to explore it.

Collins. Freedom to teach.

Published by Collins
An imprint of HarperCollins*Publishers*
The News Building
1 London Bridge Street
London
SE1 9GF

Browse the complete Collins catalogue at
www.collins.co.uk

© HarperCollins*Publishers* Limited 2015

10 9 8 7 6 5 4 3 2 1

ISBN 978-0-00-813343-6

The author asserts her moral right to be identified as the author of
this work.

British Library Cataloguing in Publication Data
A Catalogue record for this publication is available from the British Library

Publishing Manager: Tom Guy
Project Managers: Dawn Booth and Kate Ellis
Editor: Hannah Hirst-Dunton
Cover design and artwork: Amparo Barrera
Internal design concept: Amparo Barrera
Typesetter: Jouve India Private Ltd
Illustrations: Beatriz Castro, Aptara and QBS

Printed in Italy by Grafica Veneta S.p.A.

Acknowledgements

The publishers wish to thank the following for permission to reproduce content. Every effort has been made to trace copyright holders and to obtain their permission for the use of copyright materials. The publishers will gladly receive any information enabling them to rectify any error or omission at the first opportunity.

David Higham Associates Ltd for an extract from *Trouble Half-Way* by Jan Mark, Penguin Books, 1985. Reproduced by permission of David Higham Associates Ltd; Mrs A. W. Morse for an extract from "Crack-a-dawn" by Brian Morse, published in *Picnic on the Moon*, Turton and Chambers Ltd, 1990. Granted by kind permission of Mrs A. W. Morse for Megan; Carlton Books Ltd and Curtis Brown Group, Inc for the poem "Winter Morning" by Ogden Nash from *Candy is Dandy, The Best of Ogden Nash*, Carlton Books Ltd, 1994 and *Parents Keep Out, 2nd edition*, Little Brown and Co, 1951, copyright © 1962 by Ogden Nash, renewed. Reproduced by permission of Carlton Books Ltd and Curtis Brown, Ltd; HarperCollins Publishers Ltd and Aitken Alexander Associates Ltd for an extract from *Wild Swans: Three Daughters of China* by Jung Chang, published by HarperCollins, copyright © Jung Chang and Globalflair Ltd. Reproduced by permission of HarperCollins Publishers Ltd and Aitken Alexander Associates Ltd; HarperCollins Publishers Ltd and Penguin Random House for an extract from *The Phantom Tollbooth* by Norton Juster, text copyright © 1961, © renewed 1989 by Norton Juster. Reproduced by permission of HarperCollins Publishers Ltd and Random House Children's Books, a division of Penguin Random House LLC. All rights reserved; and The Society of Authors for the poem "The Highwayman" by Alfred Noyes. Reproduced by The Society of Authors as the Literary Representation of the Estate of Alfred Noyes

p. 59 David Levenson/Getty Images; p. 60 INTERFOTO/Alamy

MIX
Paper from
responsible sources
FSC™ C007454
www.fsc.org

FSC™ is a non-profit international organisation established to promote the responsible management of the world's forests. Products carrying the FSC label are independently certified to assure consumers that they come from forests that are managed to meet the social, economic and ecological needs of present and future generations, and other controlled sources.

Find out more about HarperCollins and the environment at
www.harpercollins.co.uk/green

Pupil Book 6

Comprehension

Contents

Fiction: 'Trouble Half-Way'

From 'Trouble Half-Way' by Jan Mark

Amy's father has died and her mother's new husband has moved in.

For a start, Amy never knew what to call him. She would not, like Helen, call him Daddy and she knew he did not expect her to, but Step-Daddy sounded daft, and she could hardly call him Mr Ermins. Mum did not like her calling him Richard.

'You never called your Dad Michael, did you?' Mum had said unreasonably.

Usually she just made a mumbling noise. It was easier for him: she was Amy to everyone. No one would ever have called her Daughter – not Dad, not Richard.

Mum was folding the napkins into even smaller squares ready for ironing.

'What d'you want to iron nappies for?' Richard would ask, sometimes. 'Helen won't know any different.'

'Oh, I don't know – it looks ... nicer,' Mum would say.

'But no one can see them.'

'I can see them,' Mum would retort, looking at the tottering pile of flattened napkins on the table, like a stack of sandwiches waiting to be cut into quarters. Richard would be looking at the laundry basket on the floor, full of things still waiting to be ironed.

'Life's too short,' he would say.

Now he was looking at the elastic bandage around Amy's knee.

'How's your leg?'

Mum was looking at her socks but not saying anything. The socks were gyving round her ankles because she kept tugging at them during lessons and the stretchy part was giving way. Mum ironed socks, too.

'It's not too bad,' Amy said, meaning her knee, and added carefully, because it was Richard who had asked, 'thank you.'

'What do you mean, not too bad?' Mum said, quickly. 'Has it been hurting?'

'It twinged a bit this morning when I knelt down in assembly.'

'You be careful – you want it right for Thursday.

Perhaps I ought to write a note and ask Miss Oxley to let you off games and that for the start of next week.'

'But I've got to practise,' Amy said. 'Anyway, Miss Oxley won't let me do anything I shouldn't.

She says I'm the best chance we've got if Debra isn't better.'

'What's wrong with Debra?'

'She turned her ankle on the beam on Wednesday. She came down too heavy.'

Amy noticed that Richard was staring at her over the rim of his mug.

'*Kneeling*?' he said. 'In assembly?'

'Yes.'

'Hands-together-eyes-closed-Our-Father-which-art-in-heaven?'

'Yes.'

'Good God,' said Richard.

'What did *you* do in assembly, then?' Mum demanded, unfolding the ironing board.

'Stand on one leg?'

Get started

Use a dictionary or the internet to make sure you understand and can explain all of the words in the extract. Then write sentences to answer each question. Refer to the text in your answer and use quotes when you can.

1. Why didn't Amy want to call Richard "Step-Daddy"?

2. What reason did Amy's mum give for ironing the nappies?

3. What is Amy's sister called?

4. Which body part has Amy hurt?

5. What was causing the stretchy part of Amy's socks to give way?

6. What happened to Debra?

7. What is Amy's teacher called?

8. Why does Amy's mum suggest she write a note to the teacher?

Try these

Write sentences to answer each question in your own words. Explain your answer as fully as you can.

1. Amys' mums says "You never called your Dad Michael, did you?" Was this unreasonable?

2. Why do you think Amy's mum didn't like Amy calling Richard by his name?

3. How old do you think Amy's sister is?

4. Why do you think Amy feels she should add 'thank you' when she responds to Richard asking about her leg?

5. Why do you think it is important for Amy's leg to be better for Thursday?

6. How does Amy's mum feel about Amy's injury?

7. Richard says "Hands-together-eyes-closed-Our-Father-which-art-in-heaven?". Why do you think he says this?

8. Why might Amy's mum find the situation at home stressful?

Now try these

1. Describe the character of Amy, based on what you learn in the extract.

2. Choose at least three words, phrases or images from the extract that show Amy's mum being stressed.

3. Describe the character of Richard, based on what you learn in the extract.

4. How do we know that the conversation about ironing nappies does not happen at the same time as the rest of this scene?

5. Write a diary entry as if you were Amy, reflecting on her feelings about Richard and the rest of her life at the moment. How is she feeling? What is important to her?

Fiction (traditional): 'The Discontented Fish'

'The Discontented Fish' – a Senegalese folk story

Once upon a time, in a small pool isolated from the main river, lived a colony of little fish. It was a still, muddy pool, stony and weedy, and surrounded by scraggy trees and bushes.

It was, nevertheless, a happy pool. Most of the fish were friendly and content. But there was one fish, bigger and stronger than all the others, who kept himself to himself. He was aloof and haughty whenever the others came near him.

'My good fellows,' he would say, balancing himself with his long, graceful tail as he rippled his fins gently, 'can't you see I'm trying to rest? Do please stop the commotion and respect my peace.'

'I wonder how you manage to put up with us at all,' said one of the older fish, who was becoming irritated by the big fish's constant gripes. 'I wonder why a beautiful creature like you doesn't go off to the big river and mix with the other big and important fish,' he added sarcastically.

This prompted the big fish to think further on how much too big and important he was to be living in such a small pool, and after a few days he decided to leave.

'My friend is quite right,' he thought. 'I should be far happier if I lived among fish of my own size, beauty and intelligence. How trying it is to live among these stupid little creatures! With all the rain we've been having of late the floods will soon be here, and then I'll allow myself to be swept down into the big river and out of this little pool. Then I'll be able to mix with my equals – the other big fish.'

When he told the other fish in the pool, they all agreed what a splendid idea it sounded. With solemn faces, the older fish congratulated him, saying how clever he was to think of such an idea.

There followed more days of heavy rains and, sure enough, the floods arrived. The waters swept over the little pool and, while most of the fish sheltered in the bottom of the pool, the big fish rose to the top and allowed the waters to sweep him downstream to the river. Once there he noticed how different the water tasted, and how much larger the rocks and weeds were. He sighed with anticipation of the good life that lay ahead.

He was resting for a few moments beside a large rock when he became aware of the water swirling behind him. Four or five fish, much bigger than he, passed over his head. 'Out of the way, little fellow! Don't you know this is our hunting ground?' they exclaimed harshly, as they drove him away.

He escaped into a clump of thick, tangly weed. Anxiously he peered out from time to time, not having expected this so soon after his arrival. 'They obviously didn't realise who I was,' he comforted himself, somewhat uncertainly. Presently two large black and white fish came rushing straight for him, with their fearful jaws open wide. They would surely have devoured him had he not wedged himself into a crevice in the bank, just out of their reach.

All day long he dared not move, but when night came he gingerly swam out into the black water, hoping to find some supper. Suddenly he felt a sharp nip in his tail. It was a large tiger-fish, also looking for its supper. He was about to give himself up for lost when a massive dark object (a canoe – though the fish didn't know this) passed overhead, distracting the tiger-fish just long enough for the little big fish to effect his escape.

'Alas!' he said to himself, 'why ever did I come to this terrible place? If only I could get back to my little pool I would never grumble again.' And there and then he decided to try to find, before the floods receded and it was too late, the place where he had come into the big river. Slowly he wriggled along the muddy bottom of the river, anxious not to be noticed, until he came to the point where he had first arrived. With a leap he was out of the river and into the expanse of flood-water that was surging past him. How he struggled as he tried to force his way against the swirling torrent until, at last, with his strength almost gone, he found himself back in the pool again.

There he lay – panting. Too tired to move, he looked around at the familiar landmarks. 'If only I'd known what the big river was like I would never have left the safety, comfort and friendship of our pool.'

The tiny fish continued to play and splash all around him, but never again did the big fish complain or say he was too grand to live among them – even though he may still have thought so!

Get started

Use a dictionary or the internet to make sure you understand and can explain all of the words in the extract. Then write sentences to answer each question. Refer to the text in your answer, and use quotes when you can.

1. How is the small pool described?

2. How did the little big fish behave towards the other fish?

3. How did the older fish feel about the little big fish's constant gripes?

4. What did the little big fish decide to do?

5. What type of weather did the little big fish need for his plan to work?

6. Why did the little big fish sigh when he reached the river?

7. How did the little big fish get away from the two black and white fish?

8. How did the little big fish get back into the small pool?

Try these

Write sentences to answer each question in your own words. Explain your answer as fully as you can.

1. How did the little big fish behave towards the little fish in the pond?

2. Why did the little big fish want to leave the small pool?

3. How did the little big fish feel about the older fish in the pond?

4. Do you think he knew how the older fish in the pond felt about him?

5. What do you think the little big fish thought life would be like in the river?

6. What did the little big fish do to annoy the big fish in the river?

7. What made the little big fish think that the river was a "terrible place"?

8. What lesson had the little big fish learnt?

Now try these

1. Write notes about the different feelings that the little big fish would have at different points during the story. When and why would he feel these different emotions?

2. Describe the character of the older fish in the pond, based on what you learn in the extract.

3. Explain why the moment the big fish in the river says "Out of the way, little fellow!" is a turning point in the story.

4. Look at this phrase: "How he struggled as he tried to force his way against the swirling torrent". How is this phrase effective? Explain what it adds to the story.

5. Write a longer ending for the story, using at least ten lines of dialogue between some of the little fish and older fish in the pool, discussing the little big fish's return and his new attitude. Then add a moral for the story. Why do you think this is the moral?

Non-fiction (persuasive writing): Advertisements

Advertisement 1

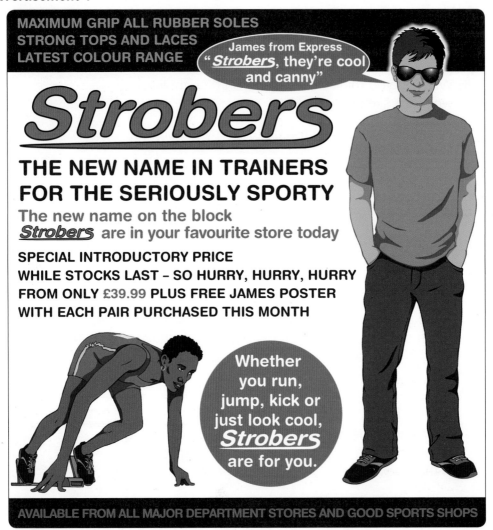

Advertisement 2

FOR SALE – STROBERS
New range of sports shoe now on sale
PRICE £40 – £70 PER PAIR

Get started

Use a dictionary or the internet to make sure you understand and can explain all of the words in the advertisements. Then write sentences to answer each question. Refer to the advertisements in your answer, and use quotes when you can.

1. What kind of product are both of these adverts promoting?

2. What is the brand name of the product?

3. Where can you buy the product?

4. What features does the product have?

5. What does James from Express say?

6. According to the adverts, who might want to buy Strobers?

7. How much do they cost?

8. What colours are used on each of the adverts?

Try these

Write sentences to answer each question in your own words. Explain your answer as fully as you can.

1. James from Express is a pop star. Why has a celebrity been used in Advert 1?

2. Why might fans of James want to buy Strobers? Give two reasons.

3. Why do you think Advert 1 tells the reader to "HURRY, HURRY, HURRY"?

4. What makes the word 'Strobers' more memorable on Advert 1 than on Advert 2?

5. Why does Advert 1 use different fonts and different colours?

6. Which advert's pricing is more likely to attract customers?

7. Why might the image of an athlete have been used on Advert 1?

8. Which advert do you think is more effective?

Now try these

1. In your own words, explain the difference between a fact and an opinion.

2. Draw a chart, lile the one shown, with two columns: 'Facts' and 'Opinions'. Write at least three things found on Advert 1 into each column of your table.

Facts	Opinions

3. Explain why the opinions in your chart have been included on Advert 1.

4. Imagine you have been asked to improve Advert 2. Write notes about what parts of the advert are effective and what parts could be made better.

5. Imagine you are a child who has seen Advert 1 and wants to persuade their parents to buy them some Strobers trainers. Write a short email as this child, giving whatever details about the trainers you think will be most effective. How much opinion and persuasive language will you use?

Non-fiction (emails): Climate change, what climate change?

Hi Grandad   23 Jun

You know I told you about this project about climate change I've got to do at school – well I'm getting a bit confused. One of my friends said it's all made up by journalists who like a good story to sell their newspapers and that the Earth isn't really warming up. He says it was really cold last winter.

Josh x

My dear Josh   23 Jun

I know we had a cold winter, but that was just in our country and in one year – but we need to look at our planet Earth overall and over several years.

Think of it like this. What happens when you go into a greenhouse on a sunny day? It's hot isn't it? That's because the glass in the greenhouse traps the heat from the sun. This carbon dioxide gas (and some others as well) that is produced when we burn oil and coal does the same in the Earth's atmosphere. That's why we call them greenhouse gases! The atmosphere acts like glass in a greenhouse. But without them, we'd freeze, so we certainly need some, but not too much of them or the planet warms more than it should.

So, with all the gases being pumped out of cars, aircraft, power stations and so on, we must be emitting more greenhouse gases and so climate change must be taking place.

Grandad x

Thanks for your email Grandad, but my friend Pete, whose dad works for an oil company, says that the temperatures on Earth have always gone up and down. That's why we had an ice age with woolly mammoths and polar bears roaming around. And now it's warm.

Josh x

Hi Josh

Pete has a point but the next ice age isn't due here for another 10,000 years. At the rate the Earth's climate and oceans are warming, the ice in the Arctic and Antarctic will have melted so much that many low-lying places will have flooded already. So we can't hang about waiting for 10,000 years, can we?

Grandad x

My dear Josh   10.30

I've been thinking more about the email you sent yesterday. Global warming? Phooey! There are some people, like Pete's dad, who say it is not happening. Can you think who some of these might be?

You guessed it! Those who use lots of fuel, who make things like cars that use lots of fuel, or actually get the fuel out of the earth – that's heavy industry, car makers and the oil, gas and coal companies. This is what people call 'vested interest'. These are people who depend on other people using lots of fuel if they are to continue making money. It's not surprising that they don't think there is any climate change. But it doesn't make them right, does it! It makes me cross!

Grandad x

16:42

You're right Grandad. I bet people from low-lying countries aren't saying we needn't be worried!

Josh x

My dear Josh   17.23

Quite so, and as your grandfather I'm worried for you and all my other lovely grandchildren. I fear there's worse to come. People who study the Earth's climate have found that as it warms up, the weather is going to get more violent and unpredictable. Hurricanes, for example, will become more powerful – a big worry for people living in the south of the United States and in the tropical Pacific or Indian Ocean areas, like the Philippines and Bangladesh. Deserts are increasing and places where lots of the Earth's food is grown, like the Great Plains of North America, will get drier. Rain will be heavier in other parts of the world so there will be more floods.

These things have already started to happen.

So even if we think there might be some doubts about some of the science, I don't think we should wait to find out, do you?

Grandad

                                                                17:41

No, Grandad, I certainly don't think we should wait!

Thank you for your help with this.

Josh x

Get started

Use a dictionary or the internet to make sure you understand and can explain all of the words in the emails. Then write sentences to answer each question. Refer to the emails in your answer, and use quotes when you can.

1. What is Josh's school project about?
2. Who is replying to Josh's emails?
3. Who said that climate change is made up by journalists?
4. Why do we need some greenhouse gases?
5. What does Pete's dad do for a living?
6. When does Grandad say the next ice age is due?
7. How many emails were sent 'yesterday'?
8. According to these emails, what is climate change?

Try these

Answer these questions in your own words. Try to support each answer with evidence from the emails.

1. Why does Josh feel confused about climate change?

2. Why do you think Pete says climate change is "made up by journalists"?

3. What reasons does Grandad give to support the idea that climate change exists?

4. What reasons does Josh give to support the idea that climate change is a myth?

5. What exactly makes Grandad cross?

6. What does "vested interest" mean?

7. How are emails different from letters?

8. Grandad always starts his emails by addressing Josh, but Josh doesn't always start his emails like this. Why do you think this might be?

Now try these

1. Describe the character of Josh, based on what you learn in the emails.

2. Do some work for Josh's project. Use the information in the emails to make a poster to inform people about climate change.

3. Pete is doing the same project as Josh, and will learn many of the same things. We know what Pete's dad has told him about climate change. Write a short diary entry as Pete, describing how he might feel about all the information he is being given.

4. Look at the email from Grandad sent at 10.30. Note down the features of this email that show you Grandad is feeling emotional about climate change.

5. Rewrite the emails as dialogue. How might you break up the emails to make the conversation sound more natural as it is spoken? Remember to use the correct punctuation for dialogue.

Poetry: 'Crack-a-Dawn'

Good day and good morning!
Here is your early morning tea
and here are your crack-a-dawn cereals.
Sugar is also provided
Breakfast in bed, room service calling!
Are you awake?
Darren, sit up I'm giving you
ten seconds, starting now! TEN.
The weather outside is fine – at least
by North Sea standards. NINE.
Just a fresh Force Six blowing and a spot
of rain lashing the rooftops. EIGHT.
The sun is shining – lucky Australians!
The bus, however, is on time
according to the local radio – SEVEN –
and if you want to walk again and be
reported to the Head that is your business
but – SIX – I have a bus to catch too
and you can pay for a taxi out of your
pocket money
if I miss it the third morning running.

FIVE. Your gerbil has been eaten by the dog
and the dog has been eaten by a crocodile
that got in down the chimney and is, at the moment,
opening its jaws over your toes –
feel it? No? Oh well.
FOUR. A letter has just arrived,
postmarked Wembley, inviting you to play
for England next Saturday against Czechoslovakia –
bet you won't be late for that. THREE.
Czechoslovakia was one of the eighteen spellings
wrong in your Geography homework.

Why wasn't it handed in last week? I found
the letter you forged from your dad
stating you had a dental appointment
on Friday afternoon – TWO – you could
at least have spelt his Christian name right
and the address. Make an appointment with him
an hour after you intend to go out tonight.

ONE. This is your mother speaking
and I am about to pour your tea
over your head, even if it causes me
extra washing. I won't begrudge the powder.
Darren, I'm giving you HALF A SECOND,
A QUARTER, AN EIGHTH.
No this is not a nightmare,
no the trickle of water you feel at this moment,
is NOT an illusion …

Brian Morse

Get started

Use a dictionary or the internet to make sure you understand and can explain
all of the words in the poem. Then write sentences to answer each question.
Refer to the poem in your answer, and use quotes when you can.

1. Who is the intended listener in this poem?

2. Who is speaking in this poem?

3. At what time of day does the poem
   take place?

4. What is the weather like outside?

5. What does the speaker say has happened to the gerbil?

6. How many spellings in total does the speaker say the listener got wrong?

7. Do you know what the listener was doing on Friday afternoon?

8. What is the speaker doing at the end of the poem?

Try these

Write sentences to answer each question in your own words. Explain your answer as fully as you can.

1. What do you think "crack-a-dawn" means?

2. Has the listener been late before?

3. Why are numbers inserted throughout the poem?

4. Why is Darren's mum trying to wake him up in a hurry?
   Give both reasons.

5. Darren's mum mentions a letter to Darren. Who does she suggest sent it?

6. What do you think Darren's mum means when she tells Darren to see his Dad "an hour after you intend to go out tonight"?

7. Why do you think Darren hadn't handed in his Geography homework?

8. How do you think Darren's mum felt before she went to wake up Darren?

Now try these

1. Describe the character of Darren, based on what you learn in the poem.

2. Darren's mum says a lot of exaggerated things to try and wake up Darren. Make notes to show which things Darren's mum says you think are true and which you think are not true. When does Darren's mum change the kinds of things she is saying?

3. Explain the effect of the numbers inserted throughout the poem.

4. Explain the effect of using long sentences in the poem.

5. Write a short poem as though Darren is writing it, responding to his mum.

Poetry: 'The Song of Hiawatha'

From 'The Song of Hiawatha' by H. W. Longfellow

'The Song of Hiawatha' is based on American Indian stories and legends. These verses are about Hiawatha's early life.

By the shining Big-Sea-Water,
Stood the wigwam of Nokomis,
Daughter of the Moon, Nokomis.
Dark behind it rose the forest,
Rose the black and gloomy pine-trees,
Rose the first with cones upon them;
Bright before it beat the water,
Beat the clear and sunny water,
Beat the shining Big-Sea-Water.

There the wrinkled, old Nokomis
Nursed the little Hiawatha,
Rocked him in his linden cradle,
Bedded soft in moss and rushes,
Safely bound with reindeer sinews;
Stilled his fretful wail by saying,
'Hush! The Naked Bear will get thee!'
Lulled him into slumber, singing,
'Ewa-yea! My little owlet!
Who is this, that lights the wigwam?
With his great eyes lights the wigwam?
Ewa-yea! My little owlet!'

Many things Nokomis taught him
Of the stars that shine in heaven;
Showed him Ishkoodah, the comet,
Ishkoodah, with fiery tresses;
Showed the Death-Dance of the spirits.
Warriors with their plumes and war-clubs,
Flaring far away to northward
In the frosty nights of Winter;
Showed the broad, white road in heaven,

Pathway of the ghosts, the shadows,
Running straight across the heavens,
Crowded with the ghosts, the shadows.

At the door on Summer evenings
Sat the little Hiawatha;
Heard the whispering of the pine-trees,
Heard the lapping of the water,
Sound of music, words of wonder;
'Minne-wawa!' said the pine-trees,
'Mudway-aushka!' said the water.

Saw the moon rise from the water,
Rippling, rounding from the water,
Saw the flecks and shadows on it,
Whispered, 'What is that, Nokomis?'
And the good Nokomis answered:
'Once a warrior, very angry,
Seized his grandmother and threw her
Up into the sky at midnight;
Right against the moon he threw her;
'Tis her body that you see there.'

Then the little Hiawatha
Learned of every bird its language,
Learned their names and all their secrets,
How they built their nests in Summer,
Where they hid them in the Winter,
Talked with them whene'er he met them,
Called them 'Hiawatha's Chickens.'
    Of all the beasts he learned the
    language,
Learned their names and all their
secrets,
How the beavers built their lodges,
Where the squirrels hid their acorns,
How the reindeer ran so swiftly,
Why the rabbit was so timid,
Talked with them whene'er he met them,
Called them 'Hiawatha's Brothers.'

Get started

Use a dictionary or the internet to make sure you understand and can explain all of the words in the poem. Then write sentences to answer each question. Refer to the text in your answer, and use quotes when you can.

1. Who is the daughter of the moon?

2. Where did Hiawatha sleep?

3. What bound him safely?

4. What did Nokomis call Hiawatha?

5. Who or what was Ishkoodah?

6. What did the pine-trees say?

7. What were "Hiawatha's Chickens"?

8. What did Hiawatha learn about beavers?

Try these

Write sentences to answer each question in your own words. Explain your answer as fully as you can.

1. What is this poem about?

2. Where does Hiawatha grow up?

3. What sounded like music to Hiawatha? What do these sounds have in common with music?

4. What is the rhythm of the poem? Be specific about how many beats and how many stresses there are in each line.

5. Why do you think an old woman might need to look after a little baby?

6. Why do you think Hiawatha called the beasts "Hiawatha's Brothers"?

7. Why do you think Hiawatha wanted to learn how to communicate with the birds and beasts?

8. Why do you think Nokomis might have told Hiawatha that the flecks on the moon were made by an angry warrior?

Now try these

1. Describe the character of Nokomis, based on what you learn in the extract.

2. Imagine that you are Hiawatha, and that you are telling Nokomis about something you have learned in the forest. Use the style and rhythm of the poem, and write seven lines from Hiawatha's point of view.

3. Find three examples of repetition in the poem. What is the effect of the repetition?

4. The sentences in the poem often have an unusual word order. Explain why you think the poet might have used the word order that he has.

5. Choose two verses from the extract and rewrite them as a description using modern language. Add extra details to the ones in the poem, and make sure you don't use the poet's unusual word order.

Poetry: 'The Highwayman'

From 'The Highwayman' by Alfred Noyes

The wind was a torrent of darkness among the gusty trees.
The moon was a ghostly galleon tossed upon cloudy seas.
The road was a ribbon of moonlight over the purple moor,
And the highwayman came riding –
    Riding – riding –
The highwayman came riding, up to the old inn-door.

He'd a French cocked-hat on his forehead, a bunch of lace at his chin,
A coat of the claret velvet, and breeches of brown doe-skin.
They fitted with never a wrinkle. His boots were up to the thigh.
And he rode with a jewelled twinkle,
    His pistol butts a-twinkle,
His rapier hilt a-twinkle, under the jewelled sky.

Over the cobbles he clattered and clashed in the dark inn-yard.
He tapped with his whip on the shutters, but all was locked and barred.
He whistled a tune to the window, and who should be waiting there
But the landlord's black-eyed daughter,
    Bess, the landlord's daughter,
Plaiting a dark red love-knot into her long black hair.

And dark in the dark old inn-yard a stable-wicket creaked
Where Tim the ostler listened. His face was white and peaked.
His eyes were hollows of madness, his hair like mouldy hay,
But he loved the landlord's daughter,
    The landlord's red-lipped daughter.
Dumb as a dog he listened, and he heard the robber say –

"One kiss, my bonny sweetheart, I'm after a prize to-night,
But I shall be back with the yellow gold before the morning light;
Yet, if they press me sharply, and harry me through the day,
Then look for me by moonlight,
    Watch for me by moonlight,
I'll come to thee by moonlight, though hell should bar the way."

He rose upright in the stirrups. He scarce could reach her hand,
But she loosened her hair in the casement. His face burnt like a brand
As the black cascade of perfume came tumbling over his breast;
And he kissed its waves in the moonlight,
    (O, sweet black waves in the moonlight!)
Then he tugged at his rein in the moonlight, and galloped away to the west.

Get started

Use a dictionary or the internet to make sure you understand and can explain all of the words in the poem. Then write sentences to answer each question. Refer to the text in your answer, and use quotes when you can.

1. At what time of day does the highwayman approach the inn?

2. What weapons was he carrying?

3. Who is Bess? What does she look like?

4. How did the highwayman signal to her that that he was there?

5. What was Bess doing at the window?

6. Who is Tim?

7. Why couldn't the highwayman kiss Bess?

8. How did Bess make contact with the highwayman instead?

Try these

Write sentences to answer each question in your own words. Explain your answer as fully as you can.

1. Why do you think the landlord's daughter was waiting at the window instead of outside the inn?

2. Why do you think the highwayman approached the inn at night, when it was shut?

3. How does the highwayman look? What might this tell you about him?

4. How does the highwayman feel about Bess?

5. How do you think Bess might feel about Tim?

6. What do you think the highwayman is going away to do?

7. What is the structure of the poem? Be specific about the lines in each verse, the beats and stresses in each line, and the rhyme scheme.

8. What is the purpose of the poem?

Now try these

1. Write notes about the different feelings that the landlord's daughter would have at different points during the story. When and why would she feel these different emotions?

2. Describe the character of the highwayman, based on what you learn in the poem.

3. Explain why you think the poet structures lines four and five of each verse in the way that he does.

4. Find one metaphor, one simile and one line showing alliteration in the poem. Make sure you understand all the words. Then explain what effects this figurative language has.

5. Write the part of the story that happens when the highwayman returns. Is it later that same night, or was there trouble? Think about how all the characters, Bess, Tim and the highwayman, have been feeling while the highwayman has been gone. Don't write the story as a poem.

Non-fiction (news report): Save it!

LATEST NEWS

Water levels at an all-time low

From our Environment Correspondent

The water companies have been given just three weeks to come up with plans to explain how they will respond to the current water shortage and to the long-term need to provide water for homes while, at the same time, protecting our rivers.

Leakage is the top priority. At present an average of 30% of treated water leaks away before it can be used.

Among the plans to be considered is for the water companies to offer to repair leaks on customers' land free of charge.

Another way of saving water is for every home to use water more carefully.

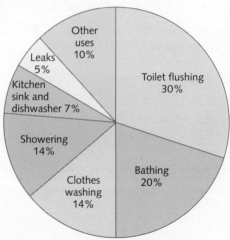

Water use in the home

A way of encouraging this would be to introduce water meters in every household. "If people knew they had to pay for every drop of water they use," said one water company spokesman yesterday, "they would soon be far more conservation minded!"

But the government is reserving its position on water meters. Apart from the extra cost of installing meters, they wonder about the fairness for people with large families, or those with medical conditions requiring frequent bathing, or those whose work makes them dirty.

As a third of domestic water currently goes down the toilet, reducing this could alone make a major impact on the immediate problem.

A recently produced Environment Agency leaflet gives some water saving tips:

- The toilet. Placing a water-filled bottle in the cistern will help by stopping the cistern from taking in so much water as it refills.

- Don't use washing machines or dishwashers with half loads.

- Showers use much less water than baths.

- Be a water pest! Snoop for dripping taps and get them fixed.

- Use washing-up water in the garden to water the flowers and vegetables, rather than fresh water.

- Use a water butt to collect rain water for the garden.

- Turn off the tap while you are brushing your teeth.

- Don't use sprinklers unless essential.

Get started

Use a dictionary or the internet to make sure you understand and can explain all of the words in the news report. Then write sentences to answer each question. Refer to the news report in your answer, and use quotes when you can.

1. Who wrote the news report?

2. How long have the water companies been given to write their plans?

3. What do the plans need to show?

4. What is the top priority?

5. What is the government position on water meters?

6. How much domestic water goes down the toilet?

7. Who has produced a leaflet giving tips on how to save water?

8. What can people do to their toilets to save water?

Try these

Write sentences to answer each question in your own words. Explain your answer as fully as you can.

1. Why has this news report been produced?

2. What effect do you think the news report is intended to have on readers? What other effects could it have?

3. Do you think the leaflet could be presented in a more effective manner? How?

4. What other images might be effective to include in the report?

5. Is it true that people would be far more conservation minded if they had to pay for every drop of water they use?

6. What does the quotation add to the report?

7. Why do you think people might waste water in their homes?

8. What is your opinion on the suggestion to install water meters?

Now try these

1. Note down at least three features that tell you this is a news report.

2. Reorganise the bullet points on the leaflet into two lists: 'Do' and 'Don't' tips.

3. Draw a chart about water meters with two sections: 'Good points' and 'Bad points'. Sort the information about water meters from the report into the correct columns of your table.

4. Write a balanced argument to respond to the question 'Should water meters be installed in every household?'.

5. Based on the information in the report, design an informative poster to help people to save water.

Non-fiction (information text): Deserts

Where are deserts located?

Few people in the world live in inhospitable deserts. Most of us live where the weather is wetter and less harsh. But almost every continent has deserts, either hot deserts or cold deserts.

The map shows where the main hot deserts are located. Notice first that there are no hot deserts in the far north or far south of the Earth. Nor are there any on the Equator. The Equator is an imaginary line around the centre of the Earth, separating the Northern Hemisphere from the Southern Hemisphere. Most of the major deserts lie in the two bands north and south of the Equator, along lines of latitude called the Tropic of Cancer and the Tropic of Capricorn.

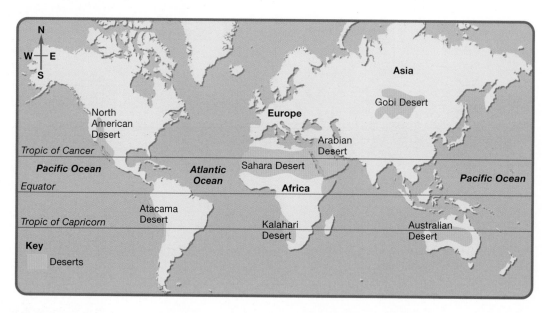

How are hot deserts formed?

The formation of hot deserts involves a lack of precipitation. Clouds form when water vapour in the air cools and forms tiny drops of water. When the drops become too heavy to stay in the air, the water falls to the ground as rain.

Usually there is water vapour in the air, but sometimes the winds bring very dry air. These winds have already lost their water vapour because they have dropped it as rain over hills and mountains, as is shown in the diagram of the west coast of the United States.

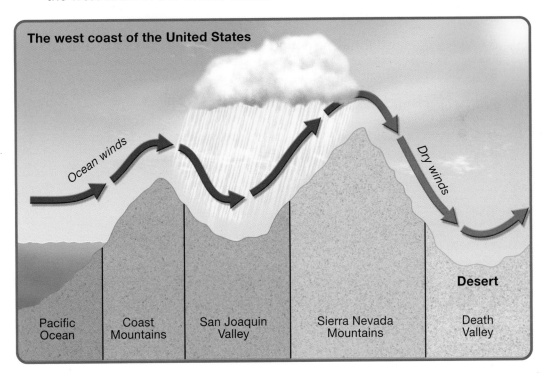

The west coast of the United States

Ocean winds

Dry winds

Desert

Pacific Ocean | Coast Mountains | San Joaquin Valley | Sierra Nevada Mountains | Death Valley

Other winds are dry because they are far from an ocean, or because they are very cold. Cold winds blowing across cold ocean currents can't collect much water vapour.

As these dry winds pass across land, no rain falls because there is no water vapour held in the air. Therefore the land remains dry and deserts are formed.

Get started

Use a dictionary or the internet to make sure you understand and can explain all of the words in the text. Then write sentences to answer each question. Refer to the text in your answer, and use quotes when you can.

1. How many people live in inhospitable deserts?

2. Are there any hot deserts in the far north of the Earth?

3. What is the Equator?

4. How many hemispheres are there?

5. Where do most of the major deserts lie?

6. In which continent is the Gobi Desert?

7. In which continent is the Kalahari Desert?

8. Why are some winds very dry? Give all three reasons.

Try these

Answer these questions in your own words. Try to support each answer with evidence from the text.

1. What are the subheadings in the extract? What might be an effective main heading?

2. On the diagram, what do the blue arrows mean? What do the red arrows mean?

3. Look at the diagram and the map. In what desert would Death Valley be found?

4. Why is the map an effective image to include?

5. From where does the air get water vapour?

6. What are lines of latitude? Work out your answer from the extract.

7. Why do you think Africa might have the largest area of hot desert land?

8. Why do you think there are few people living in deserts?

Now try these

1. Create a glossary for this text that could go in a non-fiction book about deserts. Use a dictionary for help if you need to.

2. Imagine that someone could control the wind. Write numbered instructions telling that person how to create rain.

3. Explain why the diagram "The west coast of the United States" is included in the extract.

4. In your own words, explain the content of the diagram "The west coast of the United States".

5. Create a presentation about hot deserts that you could show your class. Try to use a different structure from the one used in the extract. You could start with the wind's journey from an ocean and end with an example of a desert shown on the map.

Poetry: Views of winter

'Winter Morning' by Ogden Nash

Winter is the king of showmen,
Turning tree stumps into snowmen
And houses into birthday cakes
And spreading sugar over lakes.
Smooth and clean and frosty white,
The world looks good enough to bite.
That's the season to be young,
Catching snowflakes on your tongue.
Snow is snowy when it's snowing,
I'm sorry it's slushy when it's going.

'Winter in a Wheelchair' by Emma Barnes

Icy tyres scratch my hands,
Fingers stiff and numb,
My independence melts away,
Like a snowman in the sun.
Alone in my chair,
I watch the children play and yell,
This winter wonderland of snow,
For me is winter hell.

Get started

Use a dictionary or the internet to make sure you understand and can explain all of the words in the poems. Then write sentences to answer each question. Refer to the poems in your answer, and use quotes when you can.

1. What is the shared topic of the poems?

2. What does winter make the tree stumps become?

3. What do the houses become?

4. What kind of people catch snowflakes on their tongues?

5. What is snow like when it's going?

6. What scratches the young girl's hands?

7. How do her fingers feel?

8. With whom is she watching the children playing in the snow?

Try these

Write sentences to answer each question in your own words. Explain your answer as fully as you can.

1. How does the speaker of Ogden Nash's poem feel about winter?

2. How does the speaker of Emma Barnes's poem feel about winter?

3. Why do you think her independence disappears?

4. Why do you think independence is so important to her?

5. What is the rhyme pattern in each poem?

6. What is the effect of the line "Snow is snowy when it's snowing"? How is this effect achieved?

7. Look at the metaphors in the first three lines of 'Winter Morning'. What effects do these metaphors have?

8. Find the simile in 'Winter in a Wheelchair'. What effect does this simile have?

Now try these

1. Using 'Winter Morning' as an example, explain what personification is and how it can be effective.

2. Look carefully at the rhythm of the lines in 'Winter Morning'. One line is very different from the others. Explain why you think the poet has changed the rhythm in this line.

3. Look carefully at the rhythm of the pairs of lines in 'Winter in a Wheelchair'. One pair of lines is very different from the others. Explain why you think the poet has changed the rhythm in these lines.

4. Create a mind map that maps the words and phrases used in the poems to describe winter in both a positive way and a negative way. Then add your own positive and negative descriptions.

5. Imagine how the speaker in 'Winter in a Wheelchair' might feel having to watch her friends as they go on an exciting school trip or other day out. Using 'Winter in a Wheelchair' for help, write a short diary entry as the speaker, discussing about how she might feel while she is on her own.

Fiction: 'The Phantom Tollbooth'

From 'The Phantom Tollbooth' by Norton Juster

'It seems to me that almost everything is a waste of time,' Milo remarks as he walks dejectedly home from school. That is, until he mysteriously finds his way into the magical forest of words and numbers.

'Isn't it beautiful?' gasped Milo.

'Oh, I don't know,' answered a strange voice. 'It all depends on how you look at things.'

'I beg your pardon?' said Milo, for he didn't see who had spoken.

'I said it depends how you look at things,' repeated the voice.

Milo turned around and found himself staring at two very neatly polished brown shoes, for standing directly in front of him (if you can use the word 'standing' for someone suspended in mid-air) was another boy just about his age, whose feet were easily three feet off the ground.

'For instance,' continued the boy, 'if you happened to like deserts, you might not think this was beautiful at all.'

'For instance,' said the boy again, 'if Christmas trees were people and people were Christmas trees, we'd all be chopped down, put up in the living room, and covered with tinsel, while the trees opened our presents.'

'What does that have to do with it?' asked Milo.

'Nothing at all,' he answered, 'but it's an interesting possibility, don't you think?'

'How do you manage to stand up there?' for this was the subject that most interested him.

'I was about to ask you a similar question,' answered the boy, 'for you must be much older than you look to be standing on the ground.'

'What do you mean?' Milo asked.

'Well,' said the boy, 'in my family everyone is born in the air, with his head at exactly the height it's going to be when he's an adult, and then we all grow towards the ground.
When we're fully grown up, or as you can see, grown down, our feet finally touch. Of course, there are a few of us whose feet never reach the ground, no matter how old we get, but I suppose it's the same in every family.'

He hopped a few steps in the air, skipped back to where he started, and then began again.

'You certainly must be very old to have reached the ground already.'

'Oh no,' said Milo seriously, 'in my family we all start on the ground and grow up, and we never know how far until we actually get there.'

'What a silly system,' the boy laughed. 'Then your head keeps changing its height and you always see things in a different way? Why, when you're fifteen things won't look at all the way they did when you were ten, and at twenty everything will change again.'

'I suppose so,' said Milo, for he had never really thought about the matter.

'We always see things from the same angle,' the boy continued. 'It's much less trouble that way. Besides it makes more sense to grow down and not up. When you're very young, you can never hurt yourself falling down if you're in mid-air, and you certainly can't get into trouble for scuffing up your shoes or marking the floor if there's nothing to scuff them on and the floor is three feet away.'

Get started

Use a dictionary or the internet to make sure you understand and can explain all of the words in the extract. Then write sentences to answer each question. Refer to the text in your answer, and use quotes when you can.

1. What did Milo think was a waste of time?

2. What does Milo think is beautiful?

3. What is the first thing Milo sees when he looks for the person who had spoken?

4. How far from the ground were the boy's feet?

5. Why does the writer suggest that "standing" is not the most appropriate word to describe the boy's position?

6. According to the boy Milo meets, why might you not think the forest was beautiful?

7. At what height is the head of everyone in the boy's family, even when they are born?

8. What does the boy say is a "silly system"? Why?

Try these

Answer these questions in your own words. Try to support each answer with evidence from the extract.

1. Do you think Milo feels the forest is "a waste of time"?

2. When Milo asked, "Isn't it beautiful?", whom did he expect to answer?

3. Will the boy's feet ever reach the ground?

4. What reasons does the boy give that his way of growing makes more sense?

5. Why do you think Milo had "never really thought about" the fact that his head would keep "changing its height" as he got older?

6. When Milo says the forest is beautiful, the boy says "It all depends on how you look at things". What does he mean when he says this? What does he think Milo should consider?

7. Later, the boy says that growing upwards means "you always see things in a different way". What does he mean when he says this?

Now try these

1. Describe the character of the boy Milo meets, based on what you learn in the extract.

2. Write notes about the different feelings that Milo would have at different points during the story. When and why would he feel these different emotions?

3. Write a response from Milo to the boy, giving reasons that our way of growing makes more sense.

4. Draw a chart about the things the boy says with two sections: 'Makes sense' and 'Does not make sense'. Sort the things he says into the correct columns of your table. Remember, unusual or unfamiliar arguments can still make sense!

5. Think about the differences and similarities in meaning between the boy's sentences "It all depends on how you look at things" and "We always see things from the same angle". Explain whether or not you think the boy contradicts himself in these two sentences.

Fiction (classic): 'The Railway Children'

From 'The Railway Children' by E. Nesbit

'Please 'm,' said Ruth, 'the Master wants you to just step into the study. He looks like the dead, mum; I think he's had bad news. You'd best prepare yourself for the worst, 'm – p'haps it's a death in the family or a bank busted or –'

'That'll do Ruth,' said Mother gently, 'you can go.'

Then Mother went into the library. There was more talking. Then the bell rang again, and Ruth fetched a cab. The children heard boots go out and down the steps. The cab drove away, and the front door shut. Then Mother came in.

Her dear face was as white as her lace collar, and her eyes looked very big and shining. Her mouth looked just like a line of pale red – her lips were thin and not their proper shape at all.

'It's bedtime,' she said. 'Ruth will put you to bed.'

'But you promised we should sit up late tonight because Father's come home,' said Phyllis.

'Father's been called away – on business,' said Mother. 'Come, darlings, go at once.'

They kissed her and went. Roberta lingered to give Mother an extra hug, and to whisper:

'It wasn't bad news, Mammy, was it? Is anyone dead – or –'

'Nobody's dead – no,' said Mother, and she almost seemed to push Roberta away.

'I can't tell you anything tonight, my pet. Go dear; go *now*.'

So Roberta went.

Ruth brushed the girls' hair and helped them to undress. (Mother almost always did this herself.) When she had turned down the gas and left them she found Peter, still dressed, waiting on the stairs.

'I say, Ruth, what's up?' he asked.

'Don't ask me no questions and I won't tell you no lies,' the red-headed Ruth replied. 'You'll know soon enough.'

Late that night Mother came up and kissed all three children as they lay asleep. But Roberta was the only one whom the kiss woke, and she lay mousey-still, and said nothing.

'If Mother doesn't want us to know she's been crying,' she said to herself as she heard through the dark the catching of her mother's breath, 'we won't know it. That's all.'

When they came down to breakfast the next morning, Mother had already gone out.

'To London,' Ruth said, and left them to their breakfast.

It was nearly seven before she came in, looking so ill and tired that the children felt they could not ask her any questions. She sank into an arm-chair. Phyllis took the long pins out of her hat, while Roberta took off her gloves, and Peter unfastened her walking-shoes and fetched her soft velvety slippers for her.

When she had had a cup of tea, and Roberta had put eau-de-Cologne on her poor head that ached, Mother said:

'Now, my darlings, I want to tell you something. Those men last night did bring very bad news, and Father will be away for some time. I am very worried about it, and I want you all to help me, and not to make things harder for me.'

'As if we would!' said Roberta, holding Mother's hand against her face.

'You can help me very much,' said Mother, 'by being good and happy and not quarrelling when I'm away' – Roberta and Peter exchanged guilty glances – 'for I shall have to be away a good deal.'

'We won't quarrel. Indeed we won't,' said everyone. And they meant it, too.

'Then,' Mother went on, 'I want you not to ask me any questions about this trouble; and not to ask anybody else any questions.'

Peter cringed and shuffled his boots on the carpet.

'You'll promise this, too, won't you?' said Mother.

'I did ask Ruth,' said Peter, suddenly. 'I'm very sorry, but I did.'

'And what did she say?'

'She said I should know soon enough.'

'It isn't necessary for you to know anything about it,' said Mother; 'it's about business, and you never do understand business, do you?'

'No,' said Roberta, 'is it something to do with Government?' For Father was in a Government Office.

'Yes,' said Mother. 'Now it's bedtime, my darlings. And don't you worry. It'll all come right in the end.'

'Then don't *you* worry either, Mother,' said Phyllis, 'and we'll all be as good as gold.'

Mother sighed and kissed them.

Get started

Use a dictionary or the internet to make sure you understand and can explain all of the words in the extract. Then write sentences to answer each question. Refer to the text in your answer, and use quotes when you can.

1. Who are the characters in the extract?

2. What does Ruth think the bad news might be?

3. How does Mother look when she returns from the library?

4. Why does Phyllis protest about bedtime?

5. Who usually brushes the girls' hair?

6. How does Ruth respond to Peter's question?

7. Where did Mother go in the morning?

8. What did Peter fetch for Mother when she sat down?

Try these

Write sentences to answer each question in your own words. Explain your answer as fully as you can.

1. Why does Mother say 'That'll do Ruth,' instead of allowing Ruth to finish what she is saying?

2. What relationship to the family do you think Ruth has?

3. Why do you think Mother "almost seemed to push Roberta away"?

4. That night, how does Mother change her usual behaviour? Why do you think she does this?

5. Why do you think Roberta pretends to be asleep when Mother kisses her goodnight?

6. Why doesn't Mother want the children to ask her any questions?

7. How does Mother attempt to reassure the children? Do you think it will have worked?

8. How do you think the children feel?

Now try these

1. Describe the character of Mother, based on what you learn in the extract.

2. Write notes about the different feelings that Roberta would have at different points during the story. When and why would she feel these different emotions?

3. Mother says 'Father's been called away – on business'. What is the effect of the dash on the way this sentence might be said? What do you think that might mean?

4. Make notes about all the clues in the extract that might help you to guess what has happened. Explain what you think might have happened, based on the evidence.

5. There must be a lot of things that Roberta thinks but does not say to Mother. Write a letter as though Roberta is writing it, saying all the things she might want to say but doesn't.

Fiction (classic): 'Gulliver's Travels'

From 'Gulliver's Travels' by Jonathan Swift

Lemuel Gulliver, a ship's doctor, is the only survivor to reach the shore when his boat goes down in a great storm in 1699. Exhausted, he falls into a deep sleep.

I must have slept for a long time, for the sun had just begun to rise above the horizon when I awoke. I tried to stand up but found to my astonishment that I could not move. My hands and feet and even my hair seemed to be fastened to the ground. The sun was getting hotter. Then I was horrified to feel some small creatures moving along my left leg and up to my chest. Straining to lift my head a little, I peered down and saw a tiny human creature not much bigger than my middle finger. He was followed by about forty more of the same kind.

I was so astonished that I roared aloud. With this they all ran back in fright, and some even fell off. However, they soon returned and one climbed up to where he could get a full sight of my face.

"*Hekinah Degul!*" he called out but, although I've studied several other languages besides my native English, I could not understand what he meant.

With a violent pull, I managed to break a few of the strings that bound my left hand. I then tried to catch some of the annoying little creatures, but I could not – they ran away far too quickly.

Then one of them cried aloud, "*Tolgo Phonac!*" In an instance I felt my left hand and my face pierced with hundreds of tiny arrows. Although it was very painful, I decided not to anger my tiny captors further. I lay still and tried to think about how to get free later, when they had all gone away and left me alone.

After a little while, I heard some knocking near my right ear and the sound of a great crowd. Turning my head as far as I could, I saw that some of the tiny people were building a tower about half a metre high.

Now one little man, who seemed to be important, climbed up to the top of it and made a long speech, not a word of which I could understand. He said the word *"Lilliput"* several times, however, and I guessed that this might be the name of the place I was in. He looked quite friendly, and since I was hungry, I put my finger to my mouth to indicate this.

Before long, about a hundred inhabitants set ladders against my sides and climbed up and walked towards my mouth, carrying little baskets of food: miniature legs of lamb, tiny roasted turkeys and sides of beef. They were deliciously cooked, but three of them together made scarcely a mouthful for me.

Then someone called out, *"Peplum selam."* At this, they loosened the cords that bound me a little, so I was able to turn on my side. Before I knew it I was fast asleep. Only later did I discover that their doctors had put a sleeping potion into my food.

Get started

Use a dictionary or the internet to make sure you understand and can explain all of the words in the extract. Then write sentences to answer each question. Refer to the text in your answer, and use quotes when you can.

1. What did Gulliver realise when he woke up?

2. How big were the little people?

3. What was Gulliver's first reaction when he saw them?

4. What did the little people do after they returned?

5. How did Gulliver break the strings that bound his left hand?

6. What did Gulliver decide after the little people had fired arrows at him?

7. How did Gulliver indicate he was hungry?

8. Where does Gulliver think he might be?

Try these

Write sentences to answer each question in your own words. Explain your answer as fully as you can.

1. How many little people do you think there might be?

2. Why do you think they had tied Gulliver to the ground?

3. Why do you think a sleeping potion was put in the food?

4. Do you think Gulliver wants to hurt the little people?

5. After the little people have shot Gulliver with arrows, how do they behave towards him? Why do you think they behave this way?

6. Why do you think there isn't more description of the setting?

7. In what different ways does Gulliver refer to the little people? How do the ways he refers to them show what he thinks of them?

8. What does the phrase "only later did I discover" suggest about what happens next in this story?

Now try these

1. Describe the character of Gulliver, based on what you learn in the extract.

2. Choose and note down at least three phrases that show Gulliver isn't relying on only his sight to understand what's happening around him. What other senses are described?

3. Look at the words the little people say and when they say them. Create a glossary for this extract that explains the little people's language.

4. Look at the way the first paragraph gives information about Gulliver's situation. The author could simply have written 'When I awoke, some small creatures had tied me down.' Explain the effect of the way the first paragraph is written and how this effect is achieved.

5. What do you think the little people plan to do with Gulliver next? Write a speech for the "little man, who seemed to be important", to read from the wooden tower. Think about what plans he might have, and how he might hope to deal with the giant.

Playscript: 'Compere Lapin and Compere Tig'

SETTING

A lush green landscape with trees and a clear pool of water on a warm day

CHARACTERS

A King
Compere Lapin
Compere Tig
The King's guards
A wise man

SCENE 1

(King enters downstage left. A wise man follows closely behind him.)

KING: Ah, look at my beautiful pool. It is so lovely and fresh.
                   I cannot wait to bathe in it.

(The King bends down to look in the water. The water changes
from a clear blue to a murky colour.)

KING: (Furiously)
                   Who has been bathing
                   in my pool? The water is
                   murky and dirty!

(The wise man steps forward.)

WISE MAN: (Authoritatively)
                   O Great King, Compere Lapin is to blame. It is he
                   who dirtied the waters of your clear pool.

KING: (Thundering)
                   He must die! No-one visits my pool and lives.

(The King and wise man fade into the background (upstage left) talking together. Compere Lapin enters downstage right, looking panicked. Compere Tig also enters walking lazily in a relaxed mood.)

COMPERE LAPIN: (Whispering)
My dear friend Compere Tig, the King has a beautiful pool in his garden and he has given permission for you to bathe in it.

COMPERE TIG: (Pushing his chest out with pride)
Me? What an honour. I will make my way down to the pool.

(Compere Tig walks proudly to the pool and dips his paws in. The King sees this and cries in fury.)

KING: (Shouting)
Arrest him! I have caught the culprit. Hang him in a bag from a tree and heat a red hot iron to burn him.

(The King's guards enter downstage left. They march over to and capture Compere Tig who is struggling and crying. The guards wrap him in a bundle and tie him to a tree (downstage right). Compere Lapin watches hiding behind a rock. Stage left we can see the King's guards heating an iron rod. They remain there throughout the rest of the scene with the light on them faded. The glow of the red iron bar can still be seen.)

COMPERE TIG: (Moaning)
Help me! What am I going to do?
COMPERE LAPIN: (Running around excitedly)
Oh dear, my dear friend Compere Tig. What has happened? I am sorry to see you in such a pickle!

(The stage goes still and quiet for a moment. Compere Lapin sits washing his ears.)

COMPERE TIG: Dear friend Compere Lapin, the King is going to kill me because I refused to marry his daughter. It has nothing to do with the pool of clear water.

(Compere Lapin stops washing his ears and listens carefully.)

COMPERE LAPIN: (Sneakily)
Compere Tig, let me swap with you, I feel that it is my duty to marry the King's daughter and take this burden from you.

(Compere Lapin climbs up on the tree, releases Compere Tig and climbs into the bundle. Compere Tig hurriedly ties Compere Lapin into the bundle.)

COMPERE TIG: Ah! Compere Lapin! You have been fooled as you fooled me! Dream of your riches and glory as they will never be yours. Goodbye Compere Lapin!

(The light dims and the only thing we see is the glow from the red hot iron approaching the bundle on the tree.)

Get started

Use a dictionary or the internet to make sure you understand and can explain all of the words in the playscript. Then write sentences to answer each question. Refer to the text in your answer, and use quotes when you can.

1. What is the setting for the scene?

2. Who are the characters in the scene?

3. How does the King know that someone has been in his pool?

4. How should the actor playing the King say "He must die!"?

5. Who tells the King that Compere Lapin is to blame?

6. How does Compere Tig feel when he thinks he is allowed to bathe in the pool?

7. What do the King's guards do to Compere Tig?

8. What lie does Compere Tig tell Compere Lapin?

Try these

Answer these questions in your own words. Try to support each answer with evidence from the playscript.

1. Why does Compere Lapin enter looking panicked?

2. Why does Compere Lapin tell Compere Tig that the King has given permission for him to use the pool?

3. Why does Compere Lapin say "Compere Tig, let me swap with you"?

4. What is the relationship like between Compere Tig and Compere Lapin?

5. Do you think Compere Tig was right to trick Compere Lapin in the end?

6. Other than their names, what clues are there in the text that the characters are not humans?

7. There is no stage direction before Compere Tig's final lines. How do you think the actor playing Compere Tig should deliver these lines?

8. The stage directions say that guards heating the iron rod remain onstage throughout the scene, and that "The glow of the red iron bar can still be seen". What effect would this have for an audience?

Now try these

1. Describe the character of Compere Lapin, based on what you learn in the playscript.

2. Note down at least three features that tell you this is a playscript.

3. Write a guide for someone new to using playscripts, explaining what terms such as 'upstage', 'downstage', 'stage right' and 'stage left' mean. Use a dictionary or the internet for help if you need to.

4. Imagine you are going to perform the play. Write notes and draw pictures to show what pieces of setting, props and costumes you might need to use. Think about what might actually be possible onstage, as well as what the script says.

5. Rewrite the extract as a chapter from a story instead of a playscript. How will you explain and describe what is happening?

Non-fiction (autobiography): 'Wild Swans'

From 'Wild Swans' by Jung Chang

Jung Chang was born in Yibin, Sichuan Province in China. She wrote 'Wild Swans' partly as her autobiography and partly as a biography describing the lives of her mother and grandmother.

In the autumn of 1958, when I was six, I started going to a primary school about twenty minutes walk from home, mostly along muddy cobbled back alleys. Every day on my way to and from school, I screwed up my eyes to search every inch of ground for broken nails, rusty cogs, and any other metal objects that had been trodden into the mud between the cobbles. These were for feeding into furnaces to produce steel, which was my major occupation. Yes, at the age of six, I was involved in steel production, and had to compete with my schoolmates at handing in the most scrap iron. All around me uplifting music blared from loudspeakers, and there were banners, posters, and huge slogans painted on the walls proclaiming 'Long Live the Great Leap Forward!' and 'Everybody, Make Steel!'. Although I did not fully understand why, I knew that Chairman Mao had ordered the nation to make a lot of steel. In my school, crucible-like vats had replaced some of our cooking woks and were sitting on the giant stoves in the kitchen. All our scrap iron was fed into them, including the old woks, which had now been broken to bits.

The stoves were kept permanently lit – until they melted down. Our teachers took turns feeding firewood into them around the clock, and stirring the scraps in the vats with a huge spoon. We did not have many lessons, as the teachers were too preoccupied with the vats. So were the older, teenage children. The rest of us were organised to clean the teachers' apartments and babysit for them.

I remember visiting a hospital once with some other children to see one of our teachers who had been seriously burned when molten iron had splashed onto her arms. Doctors and nurses in white coats were rushing around frantically. There was a furnace on the hospital grounds, and they had to feed logs into it all the time, even when they were performing operations, and right through the night.

Shortly before I started going to school, my family had moved from the old vicarage into a special compound, which was the centre of government for the province. A huge furnace was erected in the parking lot. At night the sky was lit up, and the noise of the crowds around the furnace could be heard 300 yards away in my room. My family's woks went into this furnace, together with all our cast-iron cooking utensils. We did not

suffer from their loss, as we did not need them anymore. No private cooking was allowed now, and everybody had to eat in the canteen. The furnaces were insatiable. Gone was my parents' bed, a soft, comfortable one with iron springs. Gone also were the iron railings from the city pavements, and anything else that was iron. I hardly saw my parents for months. They often did not come home at all, as they had to make sure the temperature in their office furnaces never dropped.

It was at this time that Mao gave full vent to his half-baked dream … and ordered steel output to be doubled in one year – from 5.35 million tons in 1957 to 10.7 million in 1958. But instead of trying to expand the proper steel industry with skilled workers, he decided to get the whole population to take part. It was officially estimated that nearly 100 million peasants were pulled out of agricultural work and into steel production. They had been the labour force producing much of the country's food.

Get started

Use a dictionary or the internet to make sure you understand and can explain all of the words in the autobiography. Then write sentences to answer each question. Refer to the text in your answer, and use quotes when you can.

1. Where was Jung Chang born?

2. Why did she write 'Wild Swans'?

3. How old was Jung Chang when she went to primary school?

4. For what did she search on her journeys to and from school?

5. Why did she need these items?

6. What did the slogans on the walls say?

7. Who was the leader of China?

8. What replaced the cooking woks at school?

Try these

Write sentences to answer each question. Explain how or why you came up with your answer.

1. The extract is an autobiography. What is an autobiography?

2. What features of an autobiography can you find in this extract?

3. The author writes "Yes, at the age of six, I was involved in steel production". What effect does the style of this sentence have on the reader?

4. According to the extract, what was Chairman Mao's main aim for China?

5. What parts of life suffered because of this?

6. Did Jung Chang agree with Chairman Mao's plan?

7. Does the author think Chairman Mao could have increased steel production without involving the whole population?

8. Do you think Chairman Mao's plan for China is one that will have succeeded and continued? Why do you think this?

Now try these

1. Jung Chang wrote 'Wild Swans' partly as a biography of her mother. Write notes about what things in the extract affected her mother, and how they will have affected her.

2. Imagine you could interview Jung Chang. Plan six interesting questions you would like to ask her. What would you like to find out in order to understand her life better?

3. Write a dairy extract as though the child Jung Chang is writing it. Think carefully about what things make her unhappy, but also about what things she likes or doesn't mind.

4. Draw a chart, as shown, with two columns: 'Jung Chang's childhood' and 'My childhood'. Use this chart to draw comparisons between Jung Chang's experiences and your own experiences.

Jung Chang's childhood	My childhood

5. Write notes about what you would need to include if you were preparing to write your own autobiography. What parts of your childhood were interesting or important? What are you clearest memories?